Everyday Education

of related interest

The Complete Guide to Asperger's Syndrome
Tony Attwood
ISBN-13: 978 1 84310 495 7   ISBN-10: 1 84310 495 4

My Social Stories Book
Carol Gray and Abbie Leigh White
Illustrated by Sean McAndrew
ISBN-13: 978 1 85302 950 9   ISBN-10: 1 85302 950 5

Revealing the Hidden Social Code
Social Stories™ for People with Autistic Spectrum Disorders
Marie Howley and Eileen Arnold
Foreword by Carol Gray
ISBN-13: 978 1 84310 222 9   ISBN-10: 1 84310 222 6

Can I tell you about Asperger Syndrome?
A Guide for Friends and Family
Jude Welton
Illustrated by Jane Telford
Foreword by Elizabeth Newson
ISBN-13: 798 1 84310 206 9   ISBN-10: 1 84310 206 4

Different Like Me
My Book of Autism Heroes
Jennifer Elder
Illustrations by Marc Thomas and Jennifer Elder
ISBN-13: 978 1 84310 815 3   ISBN-10: 1 84310 815 1

Freaks, Geeks and Asperger Syndrome
A User Guide to Adolescence
Luke Jackson
Foreword by Tony Attwood
ISBN-13: 978 1 84310 098 0   ISBN-10: 1 84310 098 3
Winner of the NASEN & TES Special Educational Needs Children's Book Award 2003

Everyday Education
Visual support for children with autism

Pernille Dyrbjerg and Maria Vedel

Foreword by Lennart Pedersen

Jessica Kingsley Publishers
London and Philadelphia

First published in 2002 in Danish by Center for Autisme, Bagsværd, Denmark, as
Hverdagspædagogik: om visuel støtte til børn med autisme

This edition first published in 2007
by Jessica Kingsley Publishers
116 Pentonville Road
London N1 9JB, UK
and
400 Market Street, Suite 400
Philadelphia, PA 19106, USA

www.jkp.com

Library of Congress Cataloging in Publication Data
A CIP catalog record for this book is available from the Library of Congress

British Library Cataloguing in Publication Data
A CIP catalogue record for this book is available from the British Library

ISBN-13: 978 1 84310 457 5
ISBN-10: 1 84310 457 1

Printed and bound in the People's Republic of China
by Amity Printing
APC-FT4716

CONTENTS

FOREWORD

This book describes educational support aids and strategies for children with autism, in terms of visual support, visual clarification and visual structure. It is based on the coordinated work that its authors – Pernille Dyrbjerg and Maria Vedel – have carried out and on the seminars about autism they have held for parents, grandparents and professionals at the Centre for Autism in Copenhagen.

Pernille is the mother of a child with autism as well as a teacher at a specialized school for autistic children. Maria Vedel has spent most of her professional life advising parents of children with autism and other developmental disabilities. Together, the two authors aim to simplify the often complicated language and concepts of autism, in the hope of making it understandable and accessible to everyone. Although the book is aimed mainly at parents, it will also be a source of inspiration for professionals working with autistic children who wish to create an appropriately specialized environment.

Visual support aids have become a highly effective tool for use in the support of autistic children, enabling them to increase their communication and independence.

Children with autism often have a basic difficulty understanding spoken language and the social signals of body language, mime, gestures and eye contact. As adults communicating with such children, we have to express ourselves via objects, pictures, photos etc., rather than by the spoken word and the use of other non-verbal expressions. We should therefore try to communicate more simply and more clearly than normal. For example, although we may use five long sentences to explain that we are now going into town to do the shopping, one picture or object can be the basic aid that enables the autistic child to absorb the same message. The visual support aid – be it in the form of a daily diagram/schedule, any support system, communication cards etc. – has to be so simple that even non-autistic people can understand its meaning. If we do not understand these messages, we cannot expect the autistic child to do so. It should also be borne in mind that children will not want to spend much time getting to know their schedule or communication cards before being able to use them themselves. Remember that it is not real communication until everything is easier for the child, and thus for the adults around him or her. As Pernille's daughter, Dicte, said to her mother and Maria as they were collating an assortment of Dicte's visual support aids for use in this book, 'These are my signs. Before I got my signs all I could do was cry.'

Through all ages and stages of development for children, teenagers and adults, the support provided by visual systems and aids has an enormous impact. However, the shape and scale of these systems can vary. The creation of the environment within specialist education provided by, for example, dedicated pre-schools and schools for autistic children is usually based on educational principles that acknowledge the enormous importance of visual support for the children's understanding and ability to learn. However, at home, visual organization of the environment or the use of visual support systems usually needs to be individually adjusted.

In everyday life, visual support will often develop as the parents see its advantages. It is not uncommon for the desire to use visual support to arise at a time when the child is developing inappropriate or problematic behaviour. One of the arguments that both professionals and parents often make against the use of visual support systems is that they result in an over-rigid and boring daily routine for the rest of the family. This may also apply for those autistic children who are not averse to change.

However, if this does happen, it is not a question of visual support for the child. The purpose of visual support systems is to help the child have a better understanding of everyday life and to be able to communicate his or her needs – whether these involve a trip to a funfair, a wish to visit family or friends, to watch a cartoon, or to be left in peace in his or her room.

Just like all other children, teenagers and adults, people with autism differ from one another with regard to their requirement for variation in their daily lives. Some people need constant stimulation and activity, whereas others prefer a quiet daily routine.

Nonetheless, it is thought-provoking that teenagers and adults with autism or Asperger's syndrome often develop their own visual support systems, or ask for help to develop them, because they themselves have experienced the great benefit such systems can provide. These systems may be required to help them deal with quite ordinary, practical skills such as shopping, cleaning or remembering to check their appearance before leaving home. They can also be more specialized systems to help them cope with social behaviour and banter in the workplace or educational institution.

The visual support for the child with autism that we describe in this book should not be viewed as a form of treatment on its own, but rather as a strategy for help or support. In most treatment environments today there is widespread use of the specialized educational technique known as 'TEACCH'. TEACCH (Treatment and Education of Autistic and related Communication-handicapped CHildren) has developed a coherent narrative of how we can include and use visual support in what we call structured education. This kind of education also involves other important elements in the treatment of children with autism.

Visual support is a crucial part of the Picture Exchange Communication System (PECS), as it is for other methods of support such as Social StoriesTM and Comic-Strip Conversations. Behaviour-orientated programmes that use intensive interaction and speech practice as an important part of the process have also proven to be valuable in helping children with autism.

It is the opinion of the authors that no matter what method or system is being prioritized in the treatment of the autistic child, the use of visual support and visual aids will always be of such significant advantage to the child that it should not be ignored.

Creating a picture book that includes examples of visual support aids seemed an obvious thing to do. We hope that it helps other parents and professionals to understand some of the basic principles of autistic education and enables them to use some of the visual support aids for the benefit of their own children.

Lennart Pedersen
Clinical Psychologist, Centre for Autism
Bagsværd, Denmark

PREFACE

In writing this book, we hope to fill a gap in the specialist literature available, but also to inspire others to use visual support aids to reduce the problems that children with autism experience in everyday life.

The book contains many examples of the visual support used every day by Pernille's daughter Dicte. These are support aids that have been available to Dicte since she was 3 years old and that she continues to use now, aged 7. The support aids have been modified throughout Dicte's development and as her level of understanding and communication needs changed.

The book also contains examples of visual support used for children whose development has evolved somewhat differently from Dicte's. We have chosen examples that, in our experience, highlight the significant parts of the information to be communicated, thus helping the autistic child obtain an overall understanding of each situation.

By using these examples, we hope to show the variety of visual support aids possible. It is our hope that visual support will become a fundamental tool for all parents and professionals when in the company of a child with autism. We hope also that this book will serve as an inspiration for anyone who would like to get started.

It is our hope that other relatives, such as grandparents and siblings, and family friends will also find this book useful.

Pernille Dyrbjerg and Maria Vedel

INTRODUCTION

About autism

Autism is defined as a severe developmental disorder characterized by deficits in communication and language, problems with social behaviour, and repetitive and stereotypical behaviour. Asperger's syndrome is often referred to as a milder variant of autism, but it is probably more accurate to say that it is a form of autism in people with a normal level of intelligence and when early speech development has not been delayed. Children with autism and those with Asperger's syndrome often share the same basic psychological deficits, and the basic principles of their education are often also similar.

Autism cannot be cured, but many of the difficulties that this disorder creates can be eased via education, with a starting point of highlighting and clarifying the essential parts of any form of information we want to communicate to the child. Visual support aids are one of the obvious choices for this.

This need for clear information occurs in situations we have all experienced. Most people would like clear and concise instructions when given directions or when using a road map; we may need a tourist guide to tell us how to behave in unfamiliar cultures; or we may need a manual to show us how the new video machine works.

However, when communication is aimed at people with autism, the need for visual support is on a much larger scale. They require clear directions that tell them where the start and finish are in basic everyday situations – a guide to understanding the social world and a manual for functions such as getting dressed or washing themselves.

An outline of the psychological and educational consequences of autism

- The autistic child will often find it difficult to see the whole picture and therefore often focuses on details. Using pictures to represent the essential information to be communicated can help the child understand and react. For example, this can be done by organizing the physical environment (Chapter 1) or via a daily schedule and other charts to prepare the child (Chapter 2).

- The autistic child may have difficulties predicting the order of events and therefore needs a list, such as a daily schedule, as support. Breaking down activities into an ordered sequence of events can be of great assistance (see Chapter 4).

- The autistic child may have difficulties transferring experiences from one situation to another. Giving him or her a system to use can help increase independence in different situations (Chapter 5).

- The autistic child may have difficulties understanding spoken language – words that are understood in one context may not be understood in another, regardless of whether the child has good sentencing skills or does not speak at all. It is in this context that visual aids support the child's understanding of language so that he or she learns the meaning of the words more quickly.

- The autistic child may have problems understanding emotional matters, i.e. understanding and interpreting what other people think, feel and mean. Therefore the child should be taught communication and social interaction in structured situations – to enable him or her to learn the hidden social code (Chapters 6 and 7).

1.

THE PHYSICAL ARRANGEMENTS

A child who finds it difficult to comprehend the connections and meanings in his or her own world can often create personal order by, for example, wanting to watch the same part of a videotape again and again or by showing a great interest in something specific for a remarkable length of time. In this way the child tries to cope with the chaos created by confusion, by creating his or her own predictability.

The purpose of a clear physical structure is to limit the chaos for the child as much as possible and to make it easier for the child to understand what is going to happen next. The physical structure has to be simple, with an obvious message with regard to what to do and where. If possible, it is useful to have different locations for different activities. At home, there is usually a place where you eat, a place where you sleep, a place where you watch television etc. In an institution, the same place is often used for many different activities.

It is possible, both at home and in an institution, to compensate for the fact that the same location has to be used for different activities by, for example, placing a blotting pad on the table when it is being used for play, a different colour when the table is being used for homework, and a placemat at meal times. You could also attach a picture of the relevant activity on the blotting pad/placemat.

Many autistic children find it difficult to remain focused on what they are doing, and a picture can help remind them. Once the child's attention is secured, he or she is spared the interruptions of impulse actions. On reaching a particular destination, the child will then be able to match the picture with another one, or simply put it in his or her pocket to indicate that the activity has been successfully completed.

Positioning the daily schedule

Dicte's daily schedule has been positioned in a central place in the house so that she is aware of any possible changes (see Chapter 2, page 25).

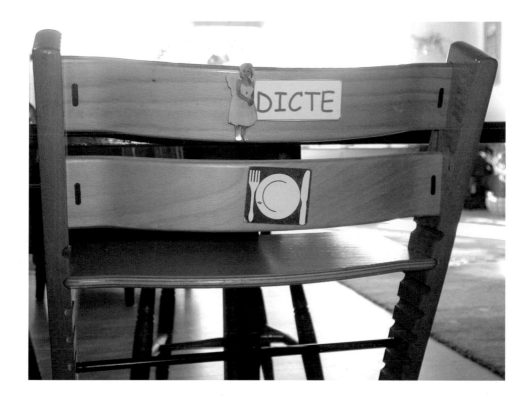

Visual support for eating

Dicte found it difficult to eat, but it became much easier for her to participate at meal times once her name was put on a chair alongside a picture of
'Eating' in a plastic pocket. Initially, she was given a picture of 'Eating' to hold,
which helped her see what she was going to do next, because there was an
identical picture on her chair and she could put her matching picture on top
of it.

Arranging a bedroom

The clear arrangement of Dicte's bedroom makes her feel safe and the room is no less comfortable than that of any other girl. The toys have been put away in drawers and boxes, which have been labelled with appropriate photos. Too much visual stimulation at one time can create 'visual noise' – and thus chaos. It may be easier to select a toy from a picture rather than choosing from open shelves.

Top: When pictures were put on Dicte's drawers and shelves and it became clear to her where her things were, she started to spend more time playing in her bedroom.

Bottom: Here a picture marks where the tape and tape recorder should be placed, so that Dicte can tidy up herself. Open bookcases with too many toys can be confusing for many children and may result in them choosing the same toy over and over again.

Dicte has a table where she can play and another one where she can work on the exercises in her boxes. The contents of her boxes vary (see Chapter 5). As autistic children often find it difficult to play on their own for any significant period of time, the assigned exercises can be put away so that the child can relax.

The door to Dicte's room is a see-through curtain. She does not like the door being closed, but it is nice for her to have some kind of boundary for her room. This enables the child to hear where the adults are, while at the same time concentrating on his or her game or exercises.

Bedtime picture

When Dicte was younger, it was very helpful for her to 'check in' with a picture for bedtime, which matched an identical bedtime picture placed in a plastic pocket on her bed. She then knew that she was going to sleep and not play when she went into her bedroom. Dicte no longer needs to match the picture, but she has asked for it to remain on the bed.

Refuge room under the stairs

It is a good idea to create a cosy space in the corner of the living room for a child who wants or needs to be near the adults. In this space, the child can have organized toys for independent play so the adults can carry on with their normal activities while the child remains under supervision. Note the tape on the floor, which encourages the child to stay within the boundaries of the assigned area.

Help in remembering where you're going

You can help children remember where they are going by handing them a picture when starting a new activity. Once the child reaches the destination (the toilet in this case), the picture is placed on the identical picture already attached beside the toilet. This makes it easier to maintain concentration and shuts out other stimuli or impulses en route.

2.

DAILY SCHEDULE

The purpose of the daily schedule is to make the day more manageable for the person with autism. The schedule needs to emphasize whether it is an ordinary day or whether there are likely to be changes. Will there be visitors, or does the shopping need to be done? Will there be a trip to the hairdresser or to the dentist?

The daily schedule is the adult's message to the child about what is going to happen during the day. A child who does not get this information will try to make his or her own plans. This can then create uncertainty and frustration for the child when these plans collide with those made by others. Too little preparation can therefore result in unnecessary problems. However, the amount of information each individual child can retain varies considerably. A child who is not very good at postponing his or her needs should perhaps be given no more than two pieces of information at a time, whereas other children can cope with information covering the entire day.

The daily schedule can contain the following:

- objects
- photographs
- pictures or drawings
- the child's own drawings
- written language, either as handwritten cards or notes on an ordinary calendar.

The form you chose depends on what makes the most sense to the child. Children may need different forms of communication at different times of their life. Small children may understand that they will have their nappy changed when shown a nappy. Older children may need to be reminded to go to the toilet by placing a picture of a toilet on the daily schedule.

The information should always be given in the usual reading direction – this means either from left to right or from the top downwards. It is fine to mix, for example, photos and physical items. The important thing is that they signal meaningful information for the child.

A daily schedule can help the child keep informed independently and, with time, to act independently of adults. In some situations, it is more dignified to know what you are going to do next, rather than constantly being given another 'instruction' without preparation.

It is the responsibility of the adult to set the daily schedule and relieve the child of the responsibility of decision making and keeping track of things.

Managing the schedule

It needs to be clear to the child how much of the schedule has been completed so far. For some, it is important to do something actively in order to keep track of where they are in the schedule. This can be done by removing the picture of the activity just completed, or by turning the picture over if it is attached by paperclips, or by crossing the activity off on a text chart.

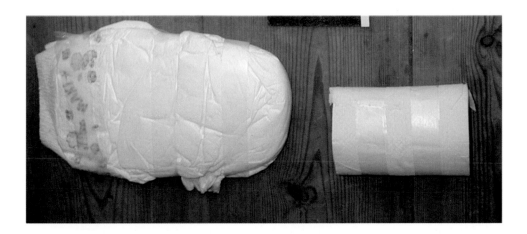

Preparing by using physical objects

The child is prepared for a change of nappy by first being shown a nappy, or by being shown a roll of toilet paper before being taken to the toilet. It is still possible that the child, just like other children, will object to having his or her nappy changed, but the preparation means that the child has understood what is about to happen, thus making the 'assault' less intrusive, rather than just being picked up and carried off.

Left: An example of a daily schedule using physical objects and a basket for the completed activities. The schedule is displayed in a central location in the home, by the front door.

Right: The same daily schedule close up. By using physical objects, you are showing and clarifying the significant message by letting the child use two senses at the same time: sight by looking at the object and touch by letting him or her feel the object.

Schedule using physical objects

Younger children or people at an early developmental stage will often derive greater benefit from being able to look at the actual objects. To see and translate pictures demands a certain understanding of symbols. Here we have used a CD shelf for the schedule.

Left: Dicte's first schedule was very simple. Dicte took the pictures from the schedule and put them in a basket when the activity was about to begin.

Right: Dicte's current schedule. The pictures now stay on the board all day. Note that there are gaps in the schedule to allow for unforeseen events. The activities of the day are shown in 'headlines'.

Left: A mobile schedule using paperclips. A mobile schedule like this one is easy to take anywhere – on visits, car journeys or to the zoo. The contents of the schedule should be adjusted according to the activities you expect the child to be able to follow.

Right: A mobile schedule made with string and pegs, with a heavy stone tied at the bottom to stabilize the string. This schedule can be hung anywhere, for example in a tent, caravan or hotel room.

Top: For older children who have a certain level of reading skills, you can use written words, for example in a normal diary. The adult writes the activities down. Later, the child/teenager can learn how to keep his or her own diary.

Bottom: The daily schedule is placed in a box located in a central place so that the person using the schedule knows where to go to stay informed. The schedule can be taken with you when you leave the house.

Scheduled break

For some children, it can be difficult not to be kept busy. It can be hard to take a break if having to make your own plans is a problem. By using a few pictures, the child can participate in choosing which activities he or she would like to relax with. Most people with autism are most comfortable with a tidy room and therefore the room used for breaks should be tidied before it is used for puzzles, sewing and computer games.

Dicte's school schedule

Dicte likes to know if it is a school day or a home day. She does not have the entire school schedule set up all at once, but has just a single day at a time. This way she does not need to expend energy trying to remember the entire course of the week.

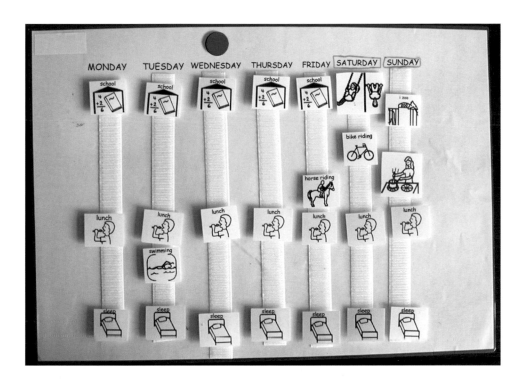

Weekly schedule

Many children need to know when they will be doing things – for example riding or swimming. They will ask again and again. Using a weekly schedule might relieve the uncertainty so that the questions are not repeated so many times. By referring to the schedule – 'You can look at the schedule if you are in doubt' – the child will learn its importance as a source of information.

Yearly schedule

All families have birthdays, celebrations and holidays, which need to be noted. A yearly schedule gives a visual overview of these events and shows the changing seasons. Dicte's schedule is colour coordinated so that she can follow the seasons. An arrow has been attached on the schedule to indicate clearly how far into the year we are. The flags mark significant birthdays.

Top: Different ways to prepare for work or play on the computer.

Bottom: Different ways to prepare for breakfast. You can have a mix of pictures and physical items. No one way is 'more correct' than another. The important thing is that the information is clear and that it is easy for the child to understand what is going to happen.

3.

PREPARING FOR SPECIAL OCCASIONS

When the child has become used to receiving information by visual aid, it becomes easier to prepare for special occasions that might otherwise be difficult to communicate to the child, e.g. holiday travel, christenings, funerals, Christmas or birthdays.

It may be possible to take autistic children to new places without preparation when they are younger, but as they get older and develop, their demands to understand their surroundings may increase. Unusual occasions can require more preparation than is necessary for events on the ordinary daily schedule.

It is important for a holiday schedule to include the number of nights you will be staying there, that you will be waiting at the airport and that you will be going home again. If the child is sensitive to noise, the preparations should include such things as the fact that the organ will be playing in the church. If the child is being looked after by grandparents or by anyone else, it is important that they also provide visual support. After all, they would not prevent the child from wearing glasses either! It is a good idea to make a mobile schedule for visits (see page 31).

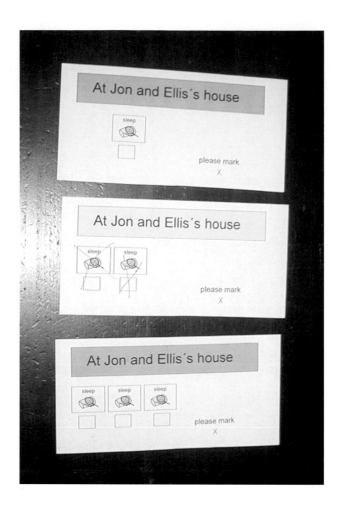

Sleeping schedule for use outside the home

The different schedules are marked with 'sleep pictures' to indicate how long Dicte is spending away from home this time. The family she is staying with will help Dicte cross off a sleep picture each morning.

Holiday schedule

The first part of the schedule describes the journey, followed by the number of nights Dicte will be sleeping there, and finally the journey home is shown – and this is the most important information of all: I will be coming home again! Dicte does not yet read the writing herself, but it is explained by the pictures, so that the information for the adults is more or less the same and the language is on a level that is appropriate for the child. A mobile schedule will then be used for the individual days ahead.

Preparing for a birthday

Left: Waiting schedule for Dicte's fifth birthday. Just as with all other children, the excitement for Dicte is great. This waiting schedule helps her to keep track of time by crossing off sleep pictures.

Right: Preparing for what is going to happen on the birthday. Out of consideration for Dicte, all activities are planned in advance: first everyone from the pre-school is coming for a visit and in the evening the family will visit.

Preparing for Dicte's seventh birthday

This time the birthday is also planned, but now Dicte has to be active herself and has to cross off the activities when they are completed. This structure means that the birthday has a greater chance of being a success.

Dicte sets the table for the birthday

To avoid confusion about who will be sitting next to whom, place cards have
been made. By involving Dicte in setting the table and placing the place cards,
she is being prepared for what is going to happen.

Unwrapping presents at the birthday

Preparation means that Dicte knows what is going to happen. Because of this, she is able to cope with so many of the neighbourhood children attending her birthday.

Advent calendar

For many autistic children, a normal advent calendar can be chaotic, as the doors are scattered all over the place in no particular order. The calendar shown here gives a clear overview of how many days remain until Christmas. The days are crossed off each morning.

Dicte and Pernille go horse riding

For a while, Pernille taught Dicte to ride. Later, Dicte joined a small group for disabled children. She has now joined a standard group for beginners at the local riding school, where the riding instructor is prepared for the possibility that once in a while Dicte will need special treatment or more detailed information that other children.

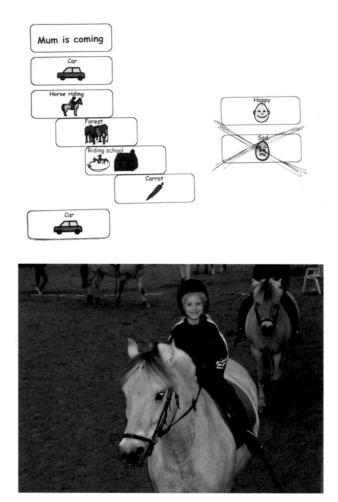

Top: The schedule was made to help Dicte get back to horse riding after a fall, when she broke her arm. As Dicte had had a fright from the fall, it was difficult for the adults to calm her down. It was easier for her to look at a picture showing her that she was now done with crying over that incident.

Bottom: After a while, horse riding once again became the favourite activity!

4.

SUPPORT FOR LEARNING NEW SKILLS

Children without autism often learn new skills by comparing themselves with others. Many autistic children do not show initiative in learning anything new, but need support to help them gain greater independence.

Autistic children also need to experience as much pleasure and dignity as possible by being able to do things on their own. Being able to carry out something independently makes them less 'people dependent'.

Once the child has learnt that 'first you do this and then this' via the daily schedule, you can transfer this system to learning new skills. Pictures or physical objects are organized in the required order, clearly showing the child what is going to happen next.

It can be difficult for the autistic child to relate experiences from one incident to another. By using a support system, the child is helped to become more flexible. For example, bath times at home and at the swimming pool are not very similar, but a support system can be the link that reinforces the similarities in the routine. Once the child – assisted by the support system – has learnt to apply the bath-time routine at the swimming pool, it may be possible for the support system to be phased out gradually.

Children who find it difficult to occupy themselves in play can often benefit from participating in domestic tasks that serve an immediate purpose. These can be things like watering plants, washing the dishes, baking etc.

Order of display using physical objects and pictures

'First supper and then watch a video.' Postponing a desired activity can be difficult for everyone. In order to accept postponement of such activities, it is important that the child knows when the activity in question will be possible and understands the order of succession of necessary and desired activities.

First dishes – then coffee

Jan can see that she will get her coffee, but first she needs to do the dishes. Being able to see the coffee cup calms Jan, and it is more dignified than having someone keep saying, 'All right, all right, you'll get your coffee!'

Support for the order of activities at the swimming pool

In Dicte's book there are nine pages showing the order of activities at the swimming pool. Most children like to go swimming but find it difficult to cope with things like having to shower and wash their hair first. The hair washing is easier to accept when it is an activity shown in the book and afterwards the red cross is moved on to more interesting activities.

Order of activity for toilet needs

For some people, it is enough to have the order of activities displayed as a reminder. Others need to move a physical marker as a transition to the next activity. The schedule can contribute as support so that the child can cope with his or her toilet needs independently and without adult supervision and control. The markers are attached with small pieces of magnetic tape.

In this example, it was important for the child to know that you put your trousers back on in the bathroom and not in the living room, where there may be guests. This time the markers are attached with Velcro tape.

Help getting dressed

Getting dressed can be done independently if the clothes are placed in the order the child has become used to: from left to right or from the top downwards. Baskets can be placed on top of each other so that the child starts with the top basket. It is easy to take a system like this to the swimming pool or to a place where the child is staying overnight.

Schedule for getting dressed

For many autistic children, the most difficult thing about getting dressed independently is keeping track of the order in which the clothes are put on. Apart from serving the purpose of helping the child keep track of getting dressed, the red markers also have a motivating purpose: it feels good finally to be able to place that last marker!

Schedule for having a bath or shower – with or without hair washing

It can be an enormous problem for some children to have their hair washed. It helps if the child knows in advance whether the bath/shower will or won't include a hair wash. The same method can be used to prepare for cutting nails or a haircut, so that the child does not experience this as an 'assault'. If the child is used to reading a schedule, this form of preparation can be very effective.

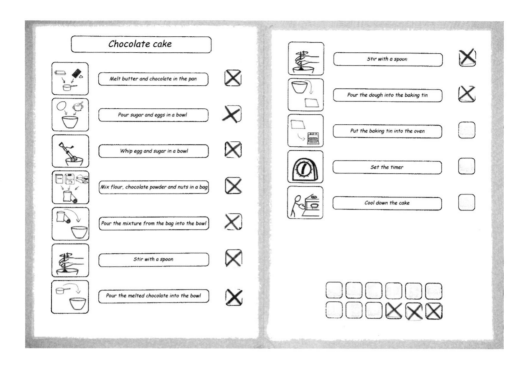

Recipe for chocolate cake

The boxes alongside the instructions are covered with red markers as the process advances. Velcro tape has been attached on both the red markers and the boxes. All recipes can be adapted like this.

Recipe for pancakes

In this scenario, the marker is moved each time the child has completed a task. If the child is allowed to move the marker, he or she will obtain an understanding of what is going to happen next. This kind of support can lead to a higher degree of independence.

Dicte cuts a banana for a fruit salad

The direction of work (seen from Dicte's perspective) is from left to right, as she's used to. The system can also be used for more complicated food preparation, e.g. a salad for the whole family.

Visual support for laying the table

The outlines of the plate, glass and cutlery have been drawn on a plastic placemat with a permanent marker. This way, laying the table can become a simple and motivating task.

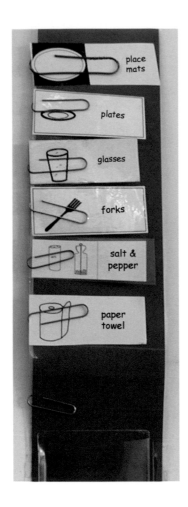
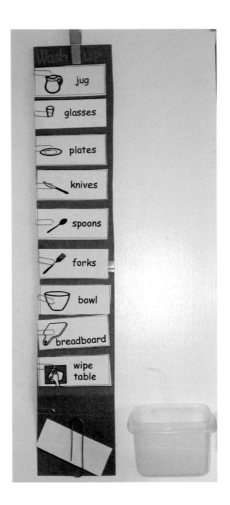

Left: A different example of visual support for laying the table. The child needs to be able to read the pictures to use this form of support.

Right: Visual support for the order in which to do the dishes. The task becomes less overwhelming when a particular order is displayed.

5.

STRUCTURED ACTIVITIES

The pictures in this chapter show ways of structuring activities that will enable children to occupy themselves independently for shorter or longer periods of time. Not all children can do this – but most of them can learn. The important things are the physical overview, shown here by using four boxes, and that the contents of the boxes (the exercises) are motivating and easy enough for the child.

The aim of the activity is not to learn anything new – that would have to be done with an adult. The aim is to be able to sit independently without being in front of the television or the computer. However, being able to sit independently is also something that has to be learnt with an adult first.

The reason for organizing the material in baskets or boxes is that the volume of exercises must not be too overwhelming for the child, and the exercises not currently being used are kept out of the way and do not distract the child. If the child does not want to do this, it is often because the exercises are still too difficult for him or her to solve alone. If at first the child cannot see the purpose of these exercises, you can put something strongly motivating in the final box – a favourite videotape or some other kind of reward.

Once the autistic child has understood this way of working and the adults remember to vary the exercises without necessarily making them more difficult, these kinds of set exercises can be very relaxing. Many children who find it difficult to initiate play will ask to do exercises.

Exercises for independent activity

Top: Boxes containing a limited number of exercises.

Bottom: The order of the work has been shown at the side of the table, by using small numbers. First the box with the number 2 is used, then the box with the number 1 box and finally the box with the number 3. The numbers on the table have Velcro tape attached on the back so that they can be used to match the numbers on the boxes. You can also choose to match colour to colour or picture to picture.

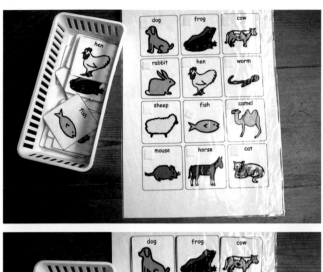

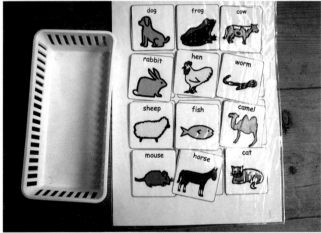

Matching exercises

The exercise here is to compare and match pictures of animals. You can use pictures from a game or, with a digital camera, make two identical copies of pictures of known objects. By using Velcro tape, the materials are fixed in place so that the child does not become frustrated by the pieces falling off.

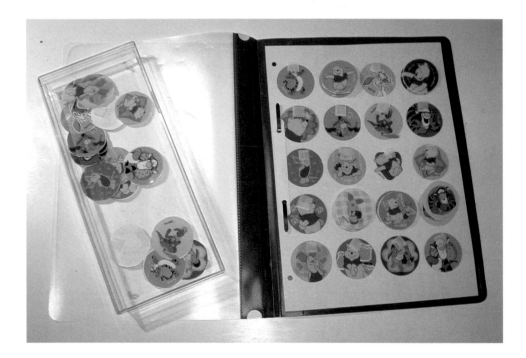

Matching familiar pictures

In this case the materials used are similar to things recognized by other children from the same age group. Here, a bit of Velcro tape has been attached to each piece in order to fix it in place so that it does not slide onto the floor. This stabilization ensures that the child does not become frustrated and does not give up too easily.

Matching numbers

Many children with autism enjoy games involving numbers, letters and word-pictures. This motivation is utilized here for an exercise that is educational and can be done independently.

Matching letters

Matching word-pictures

Matching pictures with different facial expressions

For this exercise, the material is used as an independent matching exercise. However, using the pictures in different contexts can help strengthen the child's awareness that people have different emotions, which you can read, and that emotions have different descriptions. The pictures are taken from the software program Boardmaker™.

Homemade game for matching numbers with amounts

Sorting exercises

Many autistic children crave order and structure, and enjoy sorting exercises because they allow them to create order easily. Please note that a single bead has been placed in each compartment from the beginning.

In this exercise, we have used paper pictures with Disney™ images, which the children know from cartoons. You could also use Pokémon™ images, or something else that currently occupies children of a similar age.

Sorting blocks by shape and colour

Adapting a jigsaw puzzle

Ordinary toys can often be adapted for use. Here we have used four jigsaw puzzles with different Disney™ images. The material is made more manageable by being divided into four plastic bags. Each item is placed separately on top of a laminated photocopy of the completed picture. In this example we have used a picture of Cinderella for the jigsaw puzzle.

The adult writes numbers on the back of the pieces of the Cinderella jigsaw, making it easy to solve. The child starts with the piece with the number 1 written on it, then on to number 2 etc. The orange notes support the selection, which makes it easier to select the pieces in the correct order. Rather than using plastic bags, you could place the pieces in separate baskets, as shown with the Lego™ car later in this chapter.

Simple picture-matching

This exercise is very simple and involves matching pictures. It has been set up in a way that allows the child to work on his or her own. Once again, the pieces have been attached with Velcro tape and the child moves them over to the correct position.

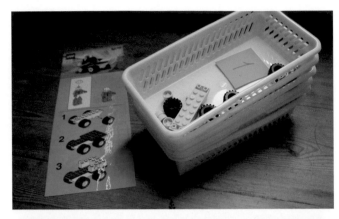

Visual pattern for building a Lego™ car

The small Lego™ boxes with building instructions are an ideal form of instruction. Note that the material is organized from left to right. If necessary, you can cut out the instructions and place the pieces in separate boxes.

Pre-school materials

Ordinary pre-school material from a stationery or toy shop is often very motivating because it is visually simple.

Bead board with prepared colours or patterns

When the squares have been coloured in beforehand, it is easy for the child to see where the beads are supposed to go. Some toy stores sell pre-coloured bead boards, but you can colour them yourself.

6.

VISUAL SUPPORT FOR COMMUNICATION

Communication is an exchange of signals. It is claimed that the majority of communication is non-verbal, which means that we mainly express ourselves and understand each other by using body language, facial expressions, tone of voice, looks and gestures.

A young non-autistic child who has not yet developed verbal language will normally communicate via gestures, which are interpreted by adults, and the child seems to have an expectation that the adults will be able to understand his or her needs.

Autistic children who have yet to learn to speak can find it difficult to understand other people's signals, as well as having problems expressing their own basic needs such as hunger, thirst and the need for care, help and comfort. Autistic children with a well-developed spoken language can experience the same difficulties. Some children can therefore benefit from carrying a key ring with a card or a picture attached to remind them that they can ask for help.

When Dicte was younger and had very limited spoken language, she communicated her need or desire for food by using pictures that had been put up on the refrigerator. First Dicte had to learn to 'hand a need' to a recipient (the adult). Slowly she learnt to communicate her needs by imitating the sounds from the adult, and little by little she learnt to express her own needs verbally. Before using picture communication, Dicte was dependent on the adult offering her food. If the adult had not 'read' her and therefore did not know that she had a request, she was left with a frustrating wait and a feeling of powerlessness.

The autistic child can also find it difficult to communicate a choice. You can train the child to choose between two things, for example by presenting two very different items and, later on, two pictures.

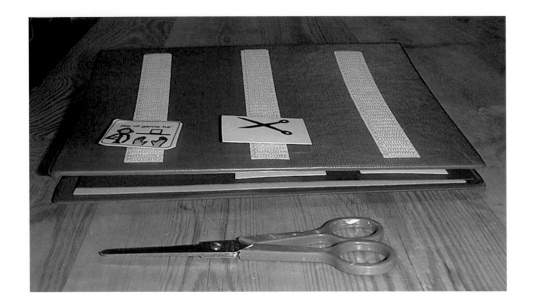

Communication system

The basic principle of the communication system is to develop the child's initiative during communication. You can organize the child's pictures, as shown above, by displaying pictures of the things the child can ask for at the time. In this case, the child can ask for a pair of scissors by handing the picture of a pair of scissors to the adult.

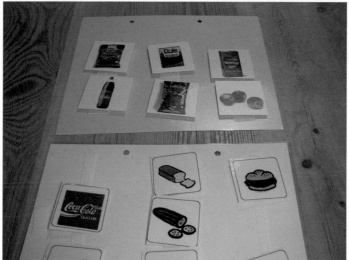

Top: A picture for the child and raisins for the adult. With the help of an adult standing behind him or her, the child practises handing a card to another adult, depending on his or her request. The basic principle is: if I want something, I need to ask for it myself by taking a card and placing it in the hand of the person who will be able to give it to me.

Bottom: The child can hand over a picture whenever he or she requires something, for example various foods.

Dicte shows how to communicate a wish or a need by handing over a picture to Maria.

Key ring with support cards

Even if they have well-developed spoken language, some autistic children are so helpless in their way of approaching people that they may find it useful to hand over a card or a picture when they need help. It can be especially difficult for the child to make verbal contact if he or she is under pressure, which is often the case if comfort or help is needed.

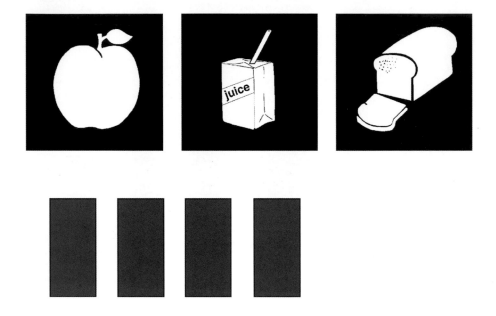

Tokens for food or drink requests

Some children who have learnt to hand over a card when they have a request can still have difficulty understanding that you cannot have an unlimited amount of food or drink. The number of tokens visually clarifies the amount of food allowed. In this case, the child can ask for something four times.

Learning to choose

Many autistic children find it difficult to choose between two things and often repeat the last thing being offered. To make it easier to learn how to choose, you can start by letting the child choose between something desirable and something irrelevant, e.g. chocolate and a cucumber. Once the child is confident with this selection process, you can let him or her choose between two equally exciting things, for example chocolate and ice-cream.

Picture selection for food from the refrigerator

Whatever is not available for selection today has been crossed out. Dicte
understands that pizza still exists, even if it is not available to her today. With
other children it may be necessary to display only pictures of the food items
currently available for selection.

Mobile selection chart made from cardboard

This chart can be taken on visits and when Dicte is staying overnight away from home. When visiting friends and family, you can phone ahead and ask what is being served.

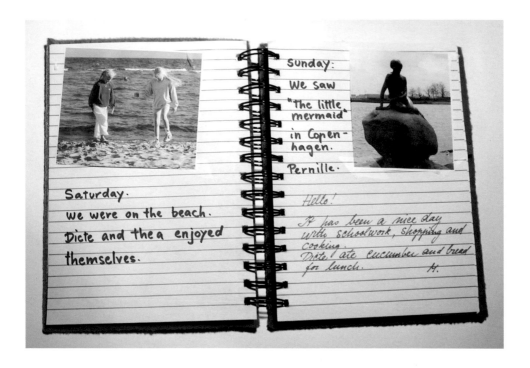

Pictures in the contact book

It is helpful for the child if a few pictures are added every day to the contact book between home and school or pre-school. If there are no pictures, it can be very puzzling for the child to understand why the parent does or does not understand things that have happened at school or pre-school. It can also be motivating for the child to participate in taking photographs for his or her own 'book of experiences' from everyday life.

7.

VISUAL SUPPORT FOR SOCIAL INTERACTION

People with autism can have great difficulties reading and, especially, interpreting social signals.

Playing a game with others normally requires the ability to:

- share attention
- imitate
- sustain a dialogue
- follow a story or an idea and be able to build on it
- take turns and be able to wait for your next turn
- adapt to others
- give and receive something from others.

Autistic children can find many of these things difficult. However, even if they don't have all of these social abilities, they can still enjoy being with other children.

You can help a child participate in social situations by creating visual clarity. During interactive play, you can clarify to the child and his or her siblings what toy belongs to whom by giving each child his or her own toy or by giving all the children identical toys on their own plastic trays. Focusing on the other child's toy can lead to the children imitating each other, or they may create another kind of interaction without the demands of social skills like sharing, taking turns or building on each other's games.

As the child develops an understanding of language, it may be possible to write supporting stories as a way of supporting the learning process for social rules and social behaviour. These stories simultaneously give verbal and visual instructions as a kind of 'social highway code'.

Playing with other children

Dicte and a friend are colouring a page each in the same colouring book. If it is too difficult for them to share the same colouring book, the problem can be solved by buying two identical colouring books.

Dicte and older sister Thea work on exercises

The exercises are of different levels of difficulty, but it is still fun to be doing the same thing!

Playing with Barbie dolls

Dicte and a friend each have their Barbie doll. The children are playing next to each other, but the fact that they have similar dolls is encouraging them to interact during the game.

Playing school

The children play school. Dicte's older sister controls the game by being the teacher and Dicte has to do the same things as the other two children.

Skipping outside

First the adult shows the children how they can skip together. Afterwards, Dicte practises with her sister and finally it becomes a game that can also be enjoyed with other children for short periods of time. The skipping rope becomes the visual indicator of what is going to happen. Skipping can be combined with counting so that it becomes motivating for children who like numbers and counting rhymes.

Dicte and Thea roller-skating

Dicte was anxious when she first tried to roller-skate and needed help to overcome this. The motivating factor for her was that she wanted to have the same equipment as her sister. This meant that she was going to have to attempt it as well.

Counting systems

Dicte is not safe outside on her own, but she is now able to be outside roller-skating with other children for short periods of time if she knows what she's doing. A counting system using Lego™ pieces has been attached to the drainpipe with Velcro tape. Each time Dicte completes a turn around the block, she comes back to put the next brick into the holder. When she gets to the last brick, a new counting system can be started.

This is a different counting system in which Dicte moves a beanbag from one bowl to another.

Taking turns dancing

Dicte's family enjoy dancing when the person wearing the hat decides how everyone is supposed to move.

In this picture, Dicte is wearing the hat. When Dicte is not wearing the hat, it is clear to her that someone else is now in charge of the dance. In this way she gains an understanding of everyone taking turns at being in charge.

Dressing-up game

Dicte and Thea like to play with dressing-up clothes when they play together. The dressing-up clothes indicate visually what games they can play, without the children being tied down to having to play something specific.

Top: Dicte and Thea play a game with Granddad.

Bottom: The red heart is placed in front of the person whose turn it is. When the turn moves on to the next person, the heart is moved in front of that person. You can also use nameplates with 'Your turn' written on them. If the heart or the nameplate distracts the child too much, you can make a small tag saying, 'Your turn'.

Top: Dicte and Thea like to sit together in front of the computer.

Bottom: This is possible because they have an egg timer and each has her own mouse mat. This way it is very clear whose turn it is and when to swap.

Picnic

Another game that works for Dicte and Thea is playing picnic. Together they pack a picnic basket, get a blanket, find a good spot and unpack everything. They might bring some juice or a doll to play with. When they have enjoyed their picnic for a while, they re-pack everything and come back home together.

Playing with bubbles

Most children enjoy blowing bubbles and it is an inexpensive pleasure. The autistic child can join in with his or her own container of soapy water. This can be a enjoyable game when other children are visiting.

Supporting stories to help with social behaviour

Stories can be used as a tool to promote communicative and social competence. You can write these stories yourself to suit the specific needs of a child.

The aim of supporting stories can be to:

- provide different options for how to act appropriately in different situations
- get used to changes and become familiar with new surroundings and events
- address problematic behaviour such as anxiety, aggression and compulsive behaviour
- increase self-awareness and strengthen friendship abilities.

When writing a supporting story bear in mind the following:

- it should be written in the first person, so that the child can experience him- or herself as the main character
- the text should be supported by pictures for children and people with a limited understanding of language
- social understanding should be encouraged in a positive manner ('I want to try' or 'I will attempt' rather than 'I don't want to' or 'I'm not allowed to')
- be aware of literal thinking and avoid words like 'always' and 'never', and instead use words like 'often', 'usually' or 'sometimes'
- it should always be adapted to the person's verbal comprehension: the use of supporting stories requires the autistic person to have some degree of verbal comprehension.

About hugs for Thea

My name is Dicte.

I am 5 years old.

I live with my mother and my father and my older sister Thea.

We are a family.

We like hugging in our family.

I like to hug Thea and most of the time Thea likes getting a hug from me.

Sometimes Thea does not feel like having a hug.

When I feel like giving Thea a hug, I can ask Thea if she wants a hug.

If Thea says, 'Yes please', then I am allowed to give her a hug.

If Thea says, 'No thank you', then I have to walk away from Thea.

Thea is not angry with me just because she does not want a hug.

If Thea says, 'No thank you', it means that she would like to wait until another time.

Thea can also tell me when she would like a hug.

My name is Sam.

I like to play games with my mother.

Sometimes the phone rings.

Then my mother goes off to talk on the telephone. This is OK.

When she has finished talking on the telephone she will come back and play with me again.

8.

PRACTICAL INFORMATION

The purpose of this book is to supply practical information about how to get started with using visual support, which many people find difficult.

The physical structure of the different supports can be very different. Whether photos, drawings, support cards, physical objects or images such as Boardmaker™ are being used depends on what communicates the clearest and most concise message to the autistic person. The picture material used should also be pleasant to work with. It can be advantageous to use detachable pictures, as this allows for flexibility and adjustment. By adding new things to the schedule and by being able to move things around, you can help the autistic person become more adaptable.

There are many examples using coloured Boardmaker™ pictures in this book. The colours on the pictures do not distract Dicte, but sometimes it is a good idea to stick with black and white illustrations – for example on schedules for getting dressed, where the colour of the clothes can vary from day to day.

We have often mentioned the importance of fixing things with Velcro tape. In our experience, this is more secure than, for example, magnetic tape. We would also like to emphasize the importance of laminating support material; the plastic cover will considerably prolong its durability.
The shelf system displaying the physical objects is a shoe rack from Ikea.

Velcro tape can be bought from a haberdashery; it needs to be sticky on both sides. Both magnetic tape and small and large paperclips can be bought from a stationery shop.

The egg timer: Egg timers are kept in most homes. However, it's important to use an old-fashioned egg timer rather than a digital one, as this visually displays how much time is remaining until something is finished. The egg
timer can be used to show when a break is over, how long someone needs to
sit at the table, or when it's time to get out of the swimming pool.

Digital/polaroid cameras: These are very useful for creating 'instant' pictures, which can then immediately be used as communication support as well as for the daily contact books, holiday albums and other experience albums. The pictures in this book have been photographed using an Olympus 2000 digital camera.

Laminating sheets: These can be bought in a stationery shop. It is often possible for support material to be laminated there as well. Most childcare institutions have laminators.

Small plastic folders: These are available in stationery shops and photo shops.

Pen and paper: It is always a good idea to have these with you and/or keep them in the car.

Small self-adhesive notepads, for example, can be suitable for drawing illustrations yourself if the need suddenly arises.

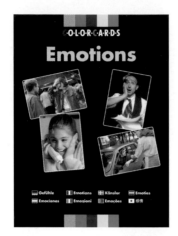

ColorCards

ColorCards® are photographic language cards using colour photographs of real objects, people, situations and activities. The card packs range from simple sets covering food and toys, through to sequence cards, for example, showing the stages of cleaning teeth. There is no text on the cards. For more information visit www.speechmark.net or contact Speechmark Publishing Ltd, Telford Road, Bicester, OX26 4LQ, UK.

Pics for PECS

These communication images are colour drawings designed to be used with the Picture Exchange Communication System (PECS), published by Pyramid Educational Consultants. The images are available as sets of laminated picture cards, or as a CD of jpeg images, which can be used with Microsoft Word and other desktop programmes. They also publish a Card Creator which provides a simple way to print off PECS pictures and other images and allows you to add or change a caption on the images as well as change the size of the pictures printed. For more information about PECS visit their website www.pecs.org.uk or www.pecs.com, or contact Pyramid Educational Consultants, Inc., 226 West Park Place, Suite, Newark, DE 19711, USA.

Pictures used with permission from Pyramid Educational Products, Inc. All rights reserved.

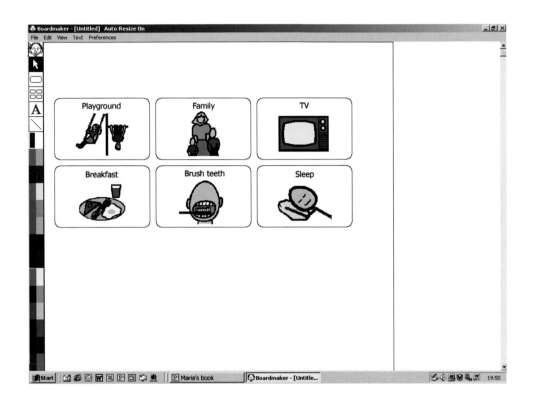

Boardmaker™

This is a graphics database containing more than 3000 pictures, which can be displayed in black and white or in colour. Some of the pictures have different levels of detail. Text lines are optional and there are various font and size choices. It is sometimes possible to insert digital pictures into Boardmaker™. The software is supplied by Mayer-Johnson Inc., PO Box 1579, Solana Beach, CA 92075, USA; phone: 858-550-0084; fax: 858-550-0449; email: mayerj@mayer-johnson.com; or visit their website at www.mayer-johnson.com. For UK suppliers, contact Widgit Software Ltd.; phone 01223 425558; or visit their website at www.widgit.com.

ISPEEK images

Janet Dixon has created a range of colour images for communicating at home and at school. *ISPEEK at Home* and *ISPEEK at School*, published by Jessica Kingsley Publishers, contain over 2000 such communication aids. The images are saved as both Windows Meta-files (WMF) and Jpegs, and can be used in Word or any desktop publishing program. The CD-Roms include some sample layouts and templates to help you set up common visual aids. For more information and freebies, visit www.ispeek.co.uk or www.jkp.com.

The images on the following pages are taken from *ISPEEK at Home* and *ISPEEK at School*. Reproduced with permission.

Laying the table

Toilet

Eating

Toilet paper

Playground

Trousers

Shower

Wash hands

Shopping trip

Dry hands

Brush teeth

Shower with hair wash

Fairground

Hair cut

Computer

Watch television

Crafts

Read a book

Go for a walk

Sleep

Medicine

Going to school

Swimming

Quiet

Getting dressed

Listening to music

Speech therapy

Washing up

Library

Empty the dishwasher

Cinema

Cooking

Bus

Dentist

Grocery shopping

Doctor

Play

Home

Bicycle

Party

Birthday cake

Ice cream

Hamburger

Zoo

Being picked up

Lunch box

Saying goodbye

Drinks flask

Going home

Family

Useful Contacts

United Kingdom

National Autistic Society
393 City Road
London, EC1V 1NG
United Kingdom
Phone: +44 (0)20 7833 2299
Fax: +44 (0)20 7833 9666
Website: www.nas.org.uk

USA

Autism Society of America
7910 Woodmont Avenue, Suite 300
Bethesda, Maryland 20814-3067
USA
Phone: +1 301 657 0881
Fax: +1 301 657 0869
Website: www.autism-society.org

RESOURCES

The following books are all published by and available from Jessica Kingsley Publishers.

Voices from the Spectrum: Parents, Grandparents, Siblings, People with Autism, and Professionals Share their Wisdom *edited by Cindy N. Ariel and Robert A. Naseef*
This book presents insights into the autism spectrum from many different perspectives – from first-hand accounts of the autistic child's school and childhood experiences to parents' and grandparents' reactions to a diagnosis. The contributors describe experiences of autism from the mildest to the most severe case, and share their methods of adapting to life on the spectrum.

The Complete Guide to Asperger's Syndrome *by Tony Attwood*
This fully comprehensive Complete Guide covers all of the key issues relating to Asperger's syndrome (AS) in depth, including diagnosis, cognitive and linguistic ability, sensory issues and areas of life that frequently present a challenge to children with AS, such as bullying at school, and to adults with AS, such as careers and relationships.

Different Like Me: My Book of Autism Heroes *by Jennifer Elder*
In this colour-illustrated book, eight-year-old Quinn, a young boy with Asperger's syndrome, introduces children aged 8 to 12 to famous, inspirational figures from the world of science, art, maths, literature, philosophy and comedy.

My Social Stories Book *by Carol Gray and Abbie Leigh White*
Taking the form of short narratives written for pre-schoolers aged from two to six, the stories in My Social Stories Book take children step by step through basic activities such as brushing their teeth, taking a bath and getting used to new clothes. The book is illustrated throughout with line drawings, which form a visual counterpart to the text.

Revealing the Hidden Social Code: Social Stories™ for People with Autistic Spectrum Disorders *by Marie Howley and Eileen Arnold*
This book, endorsed by the originator of Social Stories™, Carol Gray, offers clear and comprehensive guidance for professionals, parents and carers on how to write successful and targeted Social Stories™ that will help develop the autistic spectrum child's understanding of social interaction.

Freaks, Geeks and Asperger Syndrome: A User Guide to Adolescence *by Luke Jackson*
Drawing from his own experiences and gaining information from his teenage brother and sisters, 13-year-old Luke Jackson, who has Asperger syndrome (AS), wrote this enlightening, honest and witty book in an attempt to address difficult topics such as bullying, friendships, when and how to tell others about AS, school problems, dating and relationships, and morality.

Kids in the Syndrome Mix of ADHD, LD, Asperger's, Tourette's, Bipolar, and More! The one stop guide for parents, teachers, and other professionals *by Martin L. Kutscher, with contributions from Tony Attwood and Robert R. Wolff*
This book is a concise, scientifically up-to-date, all-in-one guide to the whole range of often co-existing neuro-behavioural disorders in children – from attention deficit hyperactivity disorder (ADHD), obsessive-compulsive disorder, and bipolar disorder, to autistic spectrum disorders, nonverbal learning disabilities, sensory integration problems, and executive dysfunction.

Different Croaks for Different Folks: All About Children with Special Learning Needs *by Midori Ochiai*
Aimed at children with autism and related spectrum conditions, this engaging colour-illustrated book explores the difficulties faced by 'frogs with a different croak'. Without using 'labels', Midori Ochiai writes about a range of conditions in a child-friendly, non-threatening way that encourages a positive and fun approach to understanding, accepting and accommodating difference.

Homeschooling the Child with Asperger Syndrome: Real Help for Parents Anywhere and On Any Budget *by Lise Pyles*
This book is packed with inspiring ideas and tips that can be used with any curriculum and on any budget. Lise Pyles explains how to design a varied study programme built around the child's own interests, making use of simple material as well as computers and online resources.

Can I tell you about Asperger Syndrome? A Guide for Friends and Family *by Jude Welton*
This illustrated book for children aged 7 to 15 is written from Adam's perspective, a young boy with Asperger syndrome (AS). He helps children understand the difficulties faced by a child with AS and tells them what AS is, what it feels like to have AS and how they can help children with AS by understanding their differences and appreciating their many talents.

ABOUT THE CENTRE FOR AUTISM

The Centre for Autism (DK) was established in 1993 with financial support from various private funds. Now granted charitable status, its goal is to promote development with regard to the diagnosis, education and treatment of people with autism, Asperger's syndrome and other related disorders.

The centre provides consultancy services for local authories, local groups, institutions and private individuals, and is currently involved in research and various development projects such as a job-training programme, diagnostic assessment, and an educational programme for parents (FUBA) with support from the Danish National Autistic Society.

Website: www.centerforautisme.dk